SCHIRMER'S LIBRARY
OF MUSICAL CLASSICS

Vol. 1887

DIMITRI SHOSTAKOVITCH

Easy Pieces for the Piano
(including two pieces for Piano Duet)

(Excerpts from music for Films, Ballets and Operettas
transcribed in simplified versions for the piano.)

Edited by
JOSEPH PROSTAKOFF

G. SCHIRMER, Inc.

DISTRIBUTED BY

HAL•LEONARD®
CORPORATION
7777 W. BLUEMOUND RD. P.O. BOX 13819 MILWAUKEE, WI 53213

CONTENTS

TWO DUETS

Easy Pieces for the Piano

Edited by Joseph Prostakoff

Dimitri Shostakovitch

1 Song of Challenge
from the film *The Contest*

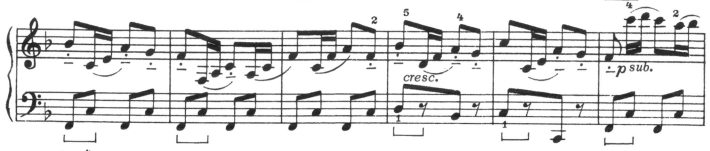

46963cx

Printed in U.S.A.

2
Lyrical Waltz
from a ballet suite

poco a poco accel.

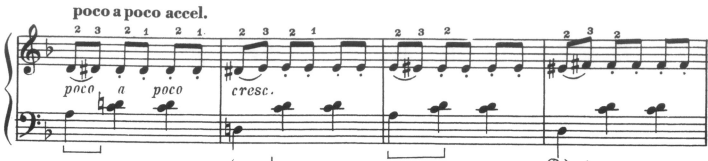

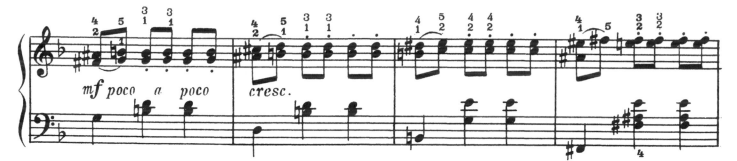

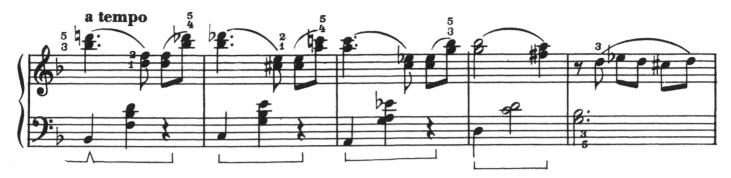

3
Gavotte
from a ballet suite

Tranquillo, leggiero

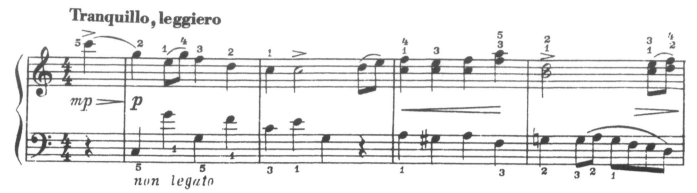

4
Romance
from a ballet suite

Moderato, espressivo

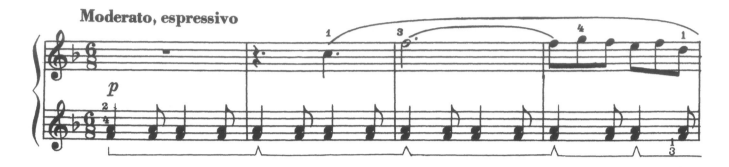

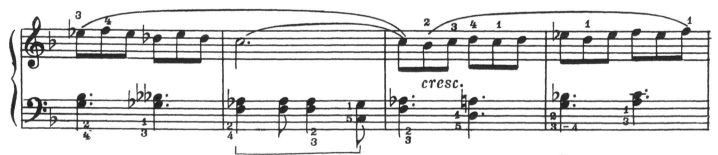

46963

rit.   a tempo

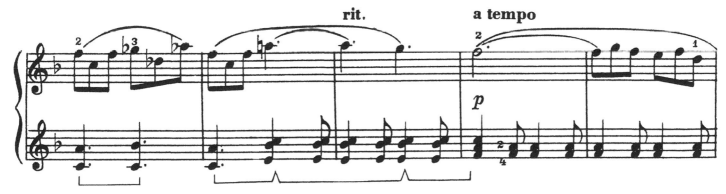

una corda

5
Waltz – A Reminiscence
from a ballet suite

Tranquillo

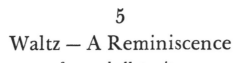

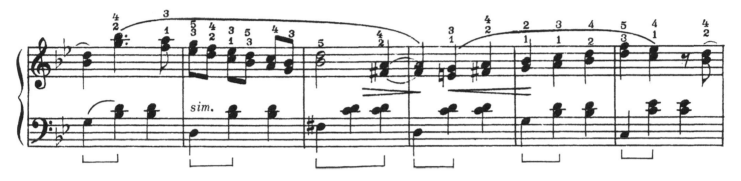
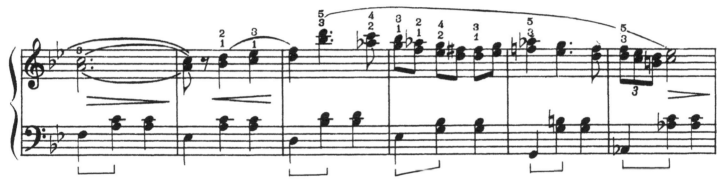

1st time: to Continue
2nd time : to Ending

ritard.

Ending **Lento**

(Ending)   *Fine* | Continue

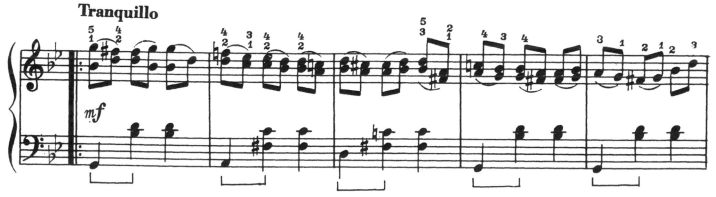

molto dim.   *pp*

Tranquillo

mf

a tempo

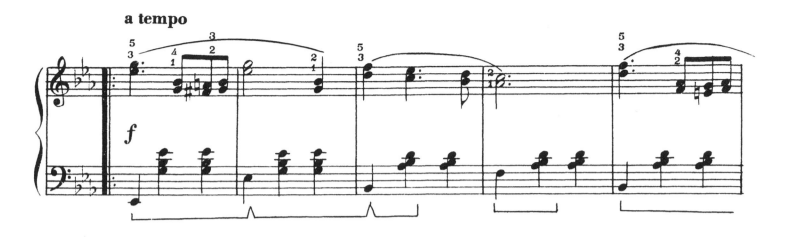

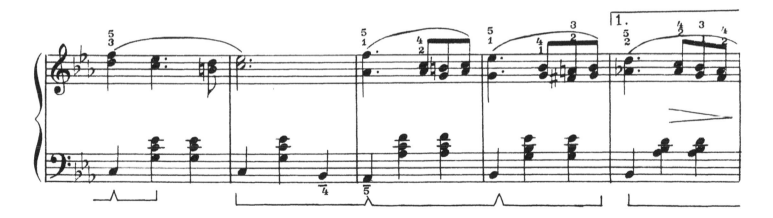

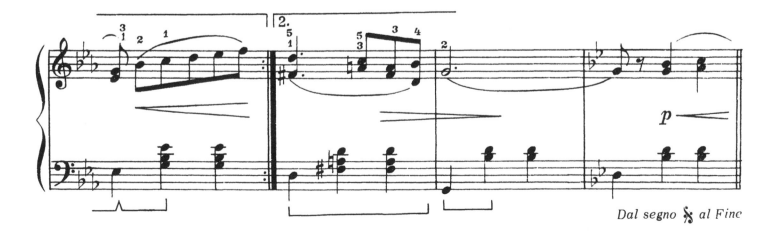

Dal segno 𝄋 *al Fine*

6
Polka
from a ballet suite

Scherzando, non troppo allegro

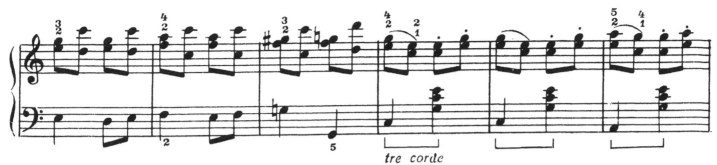

Poco più animato

Tempo I

7
Waltz Scherzo
from a ballet suite

Animato, ma non troppo allegro

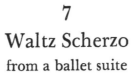

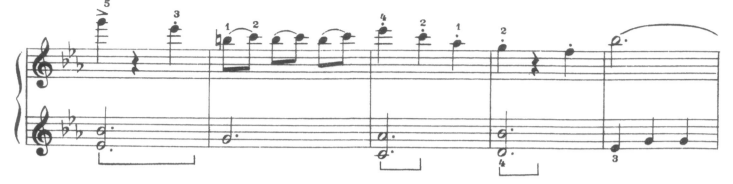

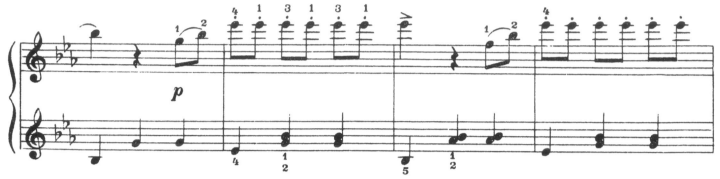

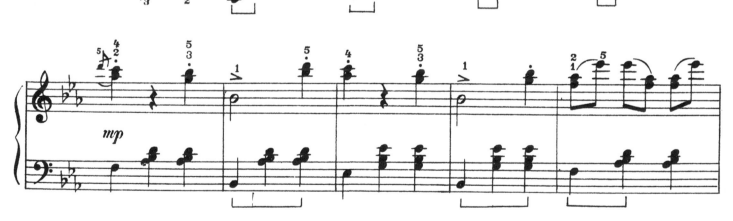

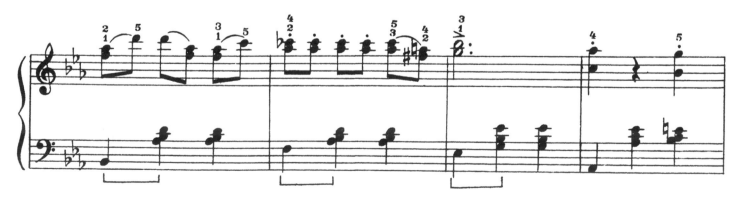

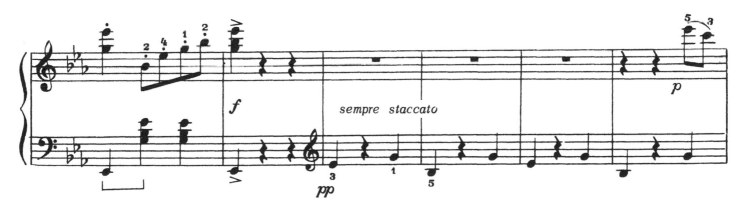

46963

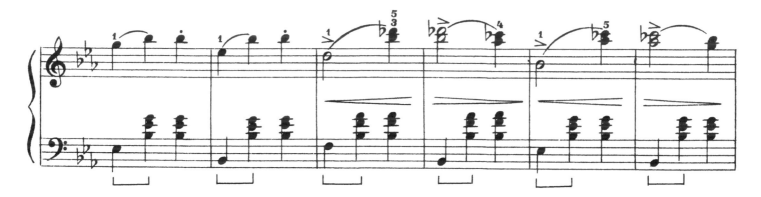

D.C. al Fine

8
Barrel-organ Polka
from a ballet suite

46963

Dal segno ℅ al Fine

9
Waltz of the Flowers
from the operetta *Moscow — The Bird Cherries*

Poco meno mosso

Dal segno 𝄋 al Fine

10
Dance
from a ballet suite

Scherzando ma non troppo allegro

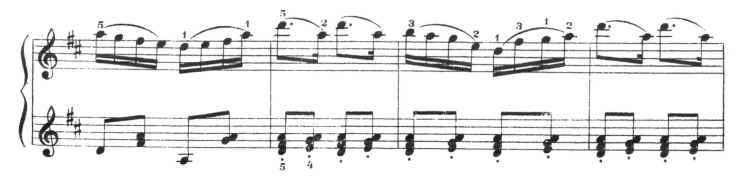

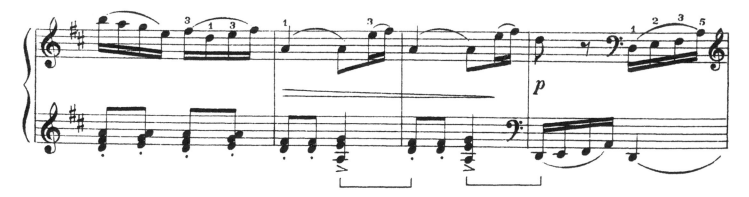

11
Lullaby
from a ballet suite

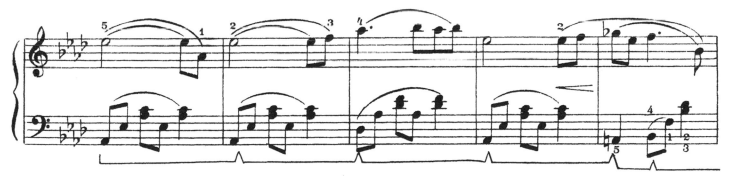

28

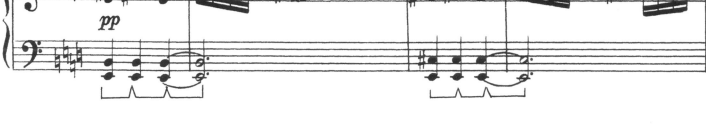

Dal segno %% al Fine

46963

12
Springtime Waltz
from the film *Mitchourin*

13
Country Dance
from the film *The Gadfly*

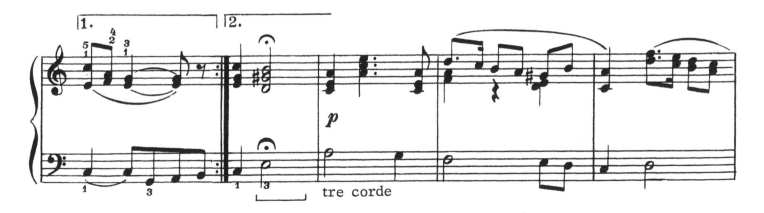

Fine

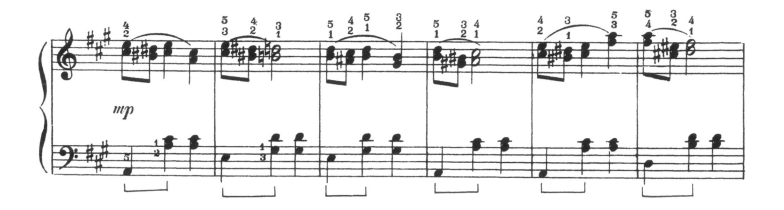

mp

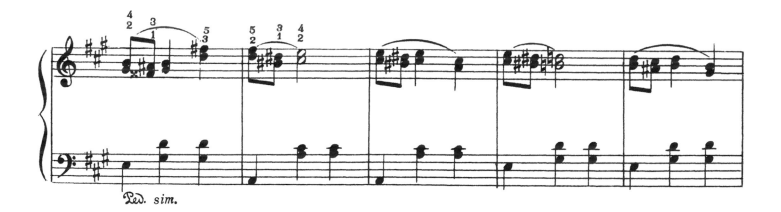

Ped. sim.

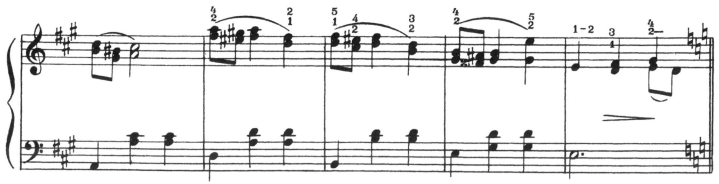

D.C. al Fine

14
Spanish Dance
from the film *The Gadfly*

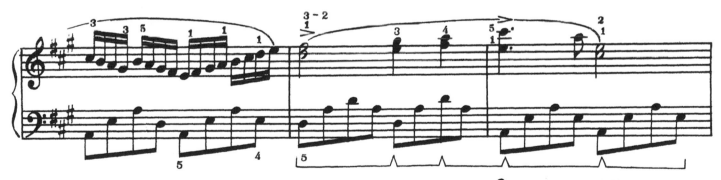

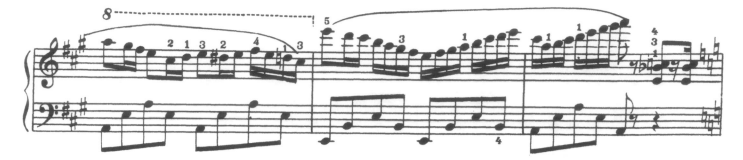

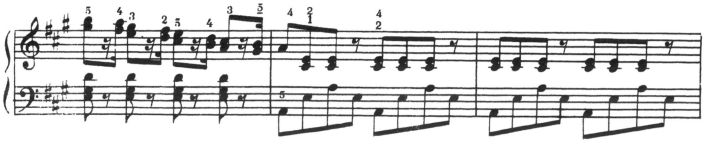

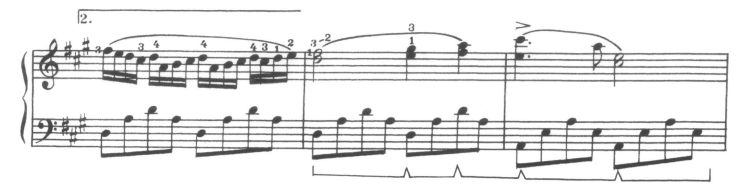

15
Nocturne
from the film *The Gadfly*

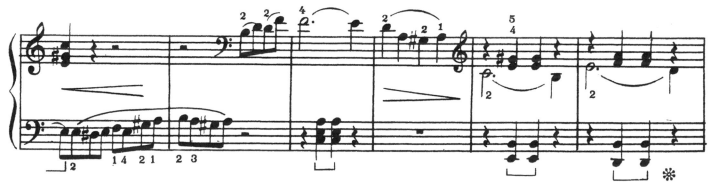

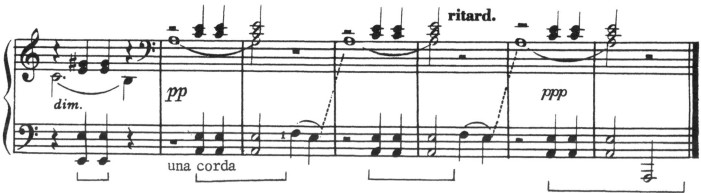

16
Barrel-organ Waltz

from the film *The Gadfly*

40

Continue

sempre stacc.

mf

marcato

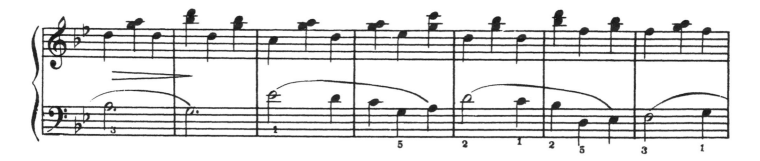

p

Dal segno 𝄋 al Fine

17
A Little Piece
from the film *The Gadfly*

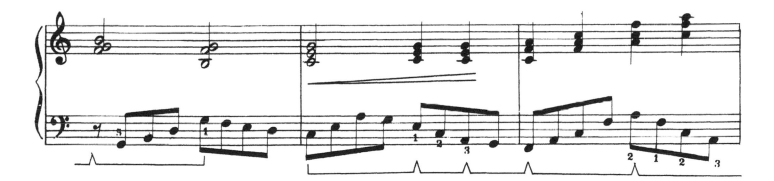

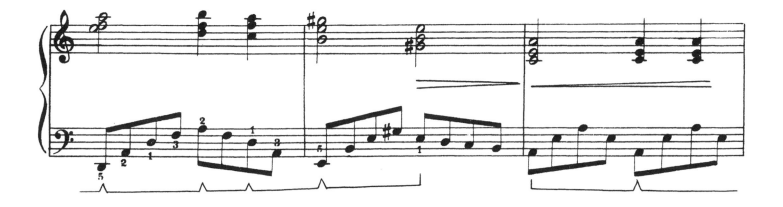

1st time : to Continue
2nd time : to Ending

Dal segno 𝄋 al Fine

18
Sentimental Waltz
from a ballet suite

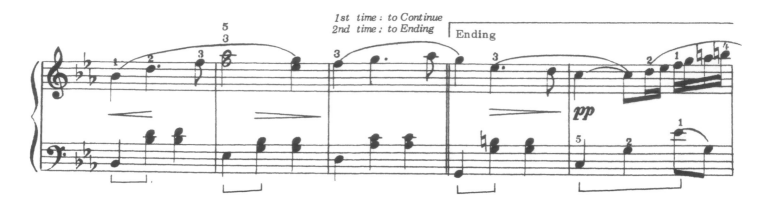

1st time : to Continue
2nd time : to Ending

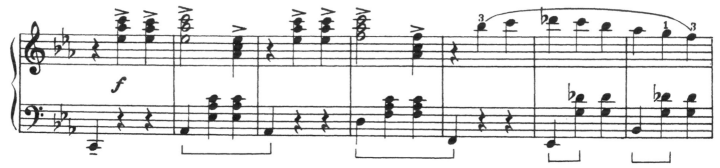

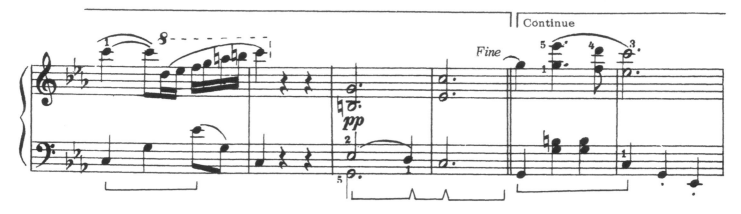

Dal segno 𝄋 al Fine

19
Skipping Dance
from a ballet suite

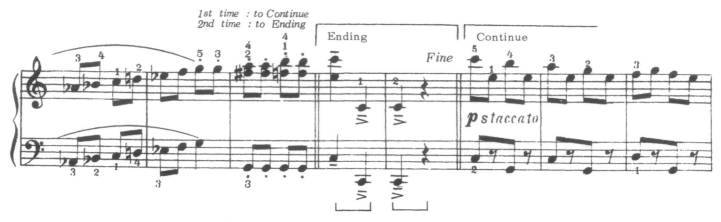

1st time : to Continue
2nd time : to Ending

Ending   Continue
Fine

p staccato

Dal segno ℅ al Fine

20
Waltz Song
from the operetta *Moscow — The Bird Cherries*

46963

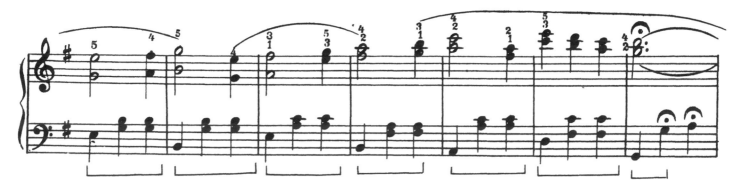

Meno mosso

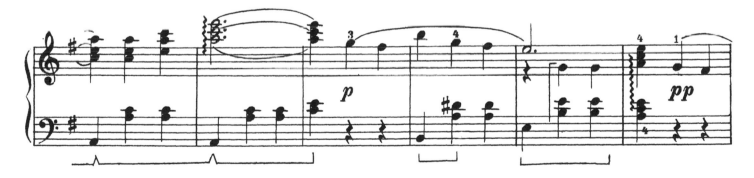

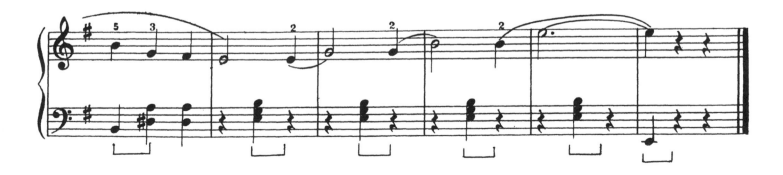

21
Nocturne
from a ballet suite

Moderato

un poco agitato

22
Melancholy Ditty
from the operetta *Moscow — The Bird Cherries*

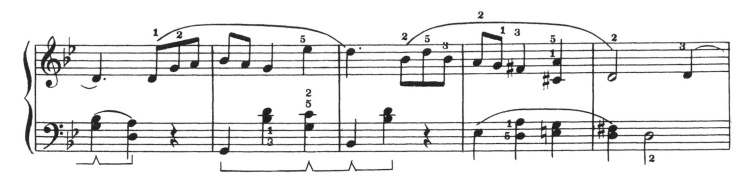

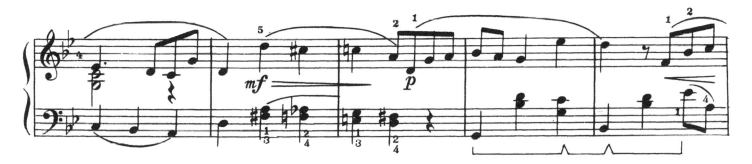

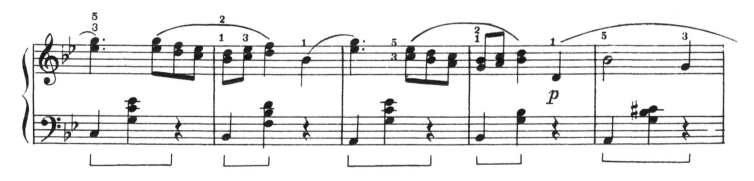

una corda

23
Dance
from a ballet suite

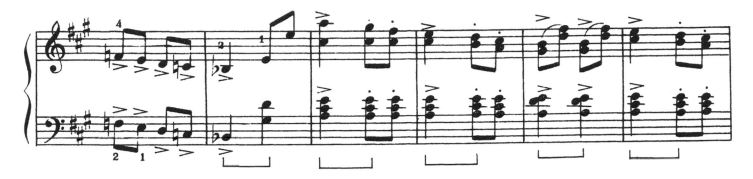

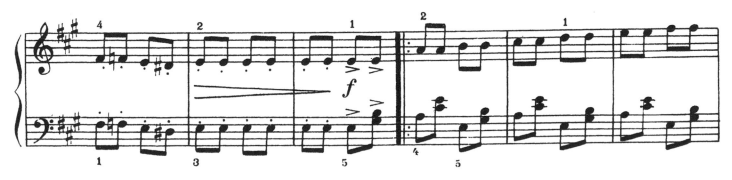

46963

24
Adagio
from a ballet suite

46963

Un poco più mosso

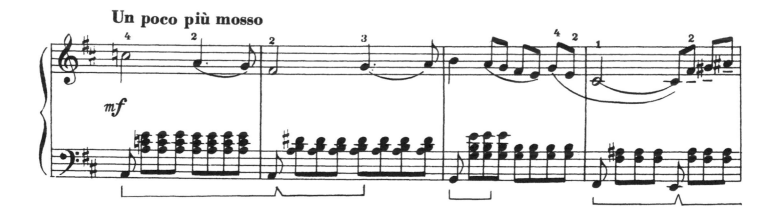

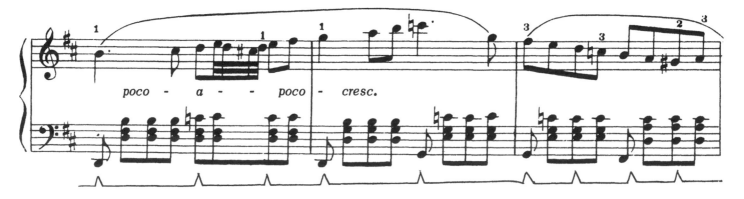

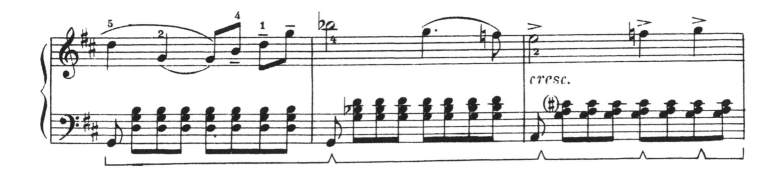

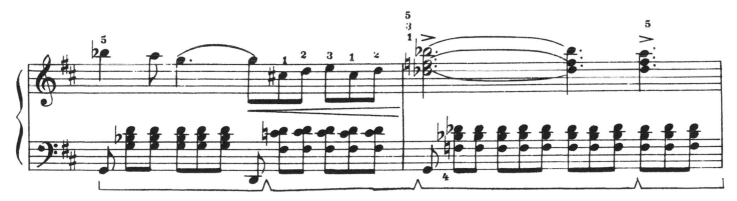

46963

una corda

25
Festival Waltz
from a ballet suite

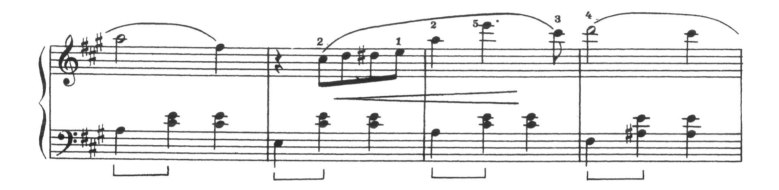

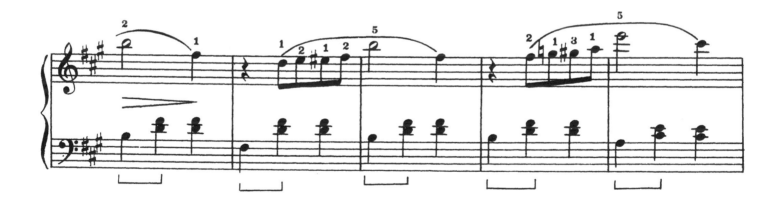

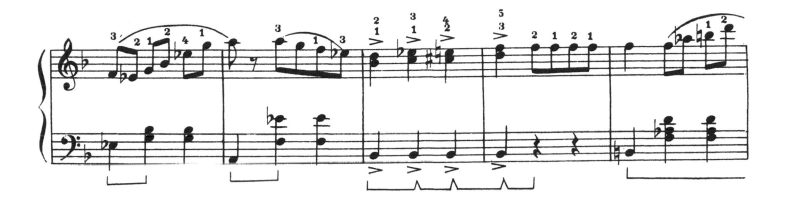

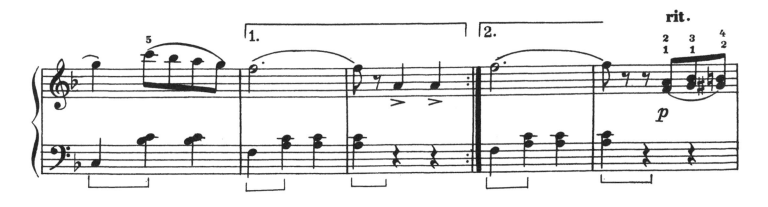

a tempo

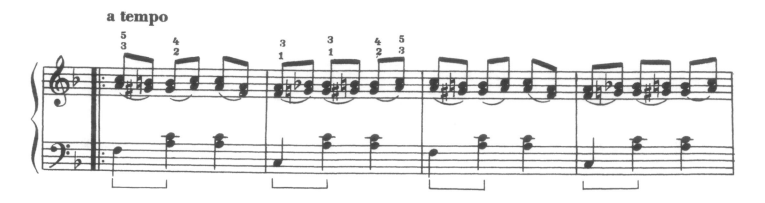

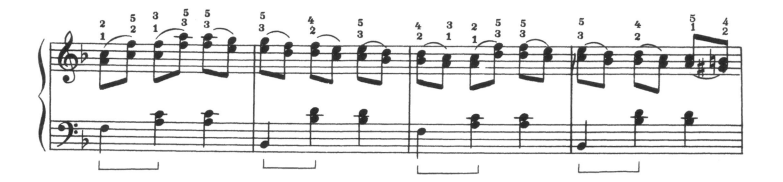

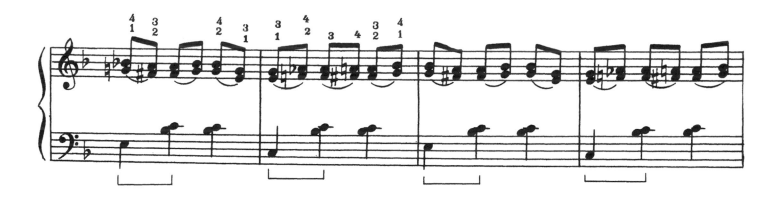

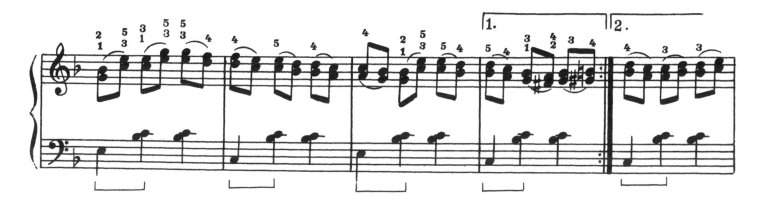

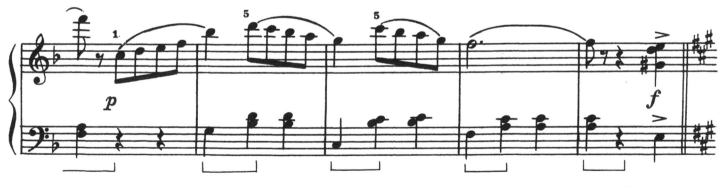

Dal segno 𝄋 al Fine

TWO DUETS

1. Waltz

from the film *Unity*

Secondo

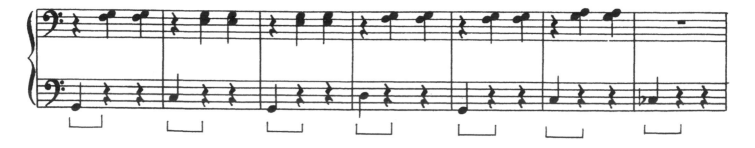

TWO DUETS

1. Waltz

from the film *Unity*

Primo

Secondo

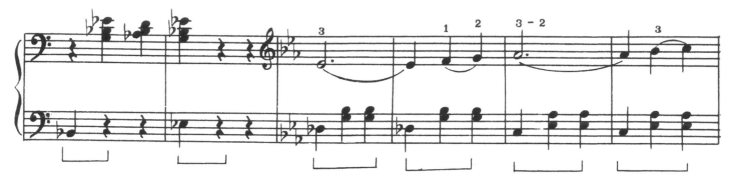

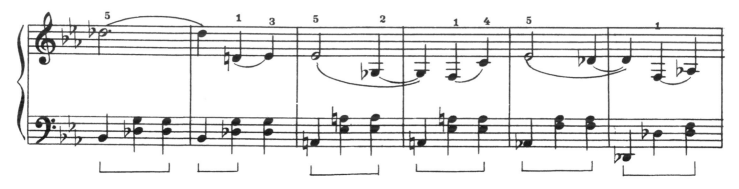

a tempo

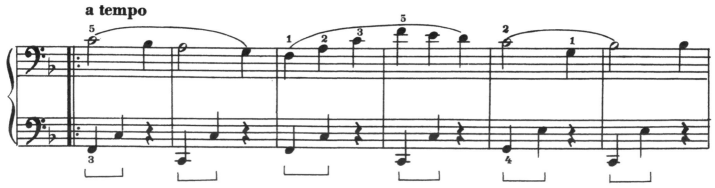

Primo

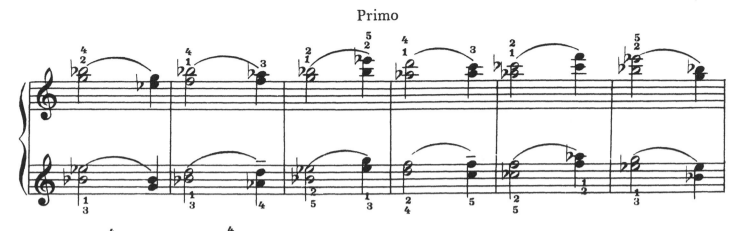

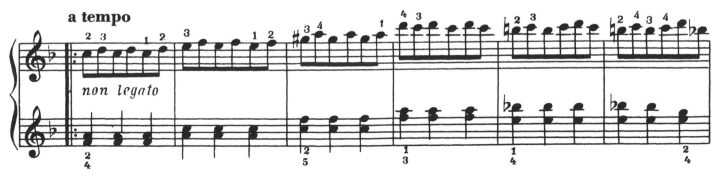

Secondo

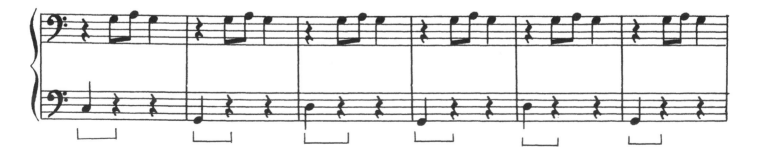

Primo

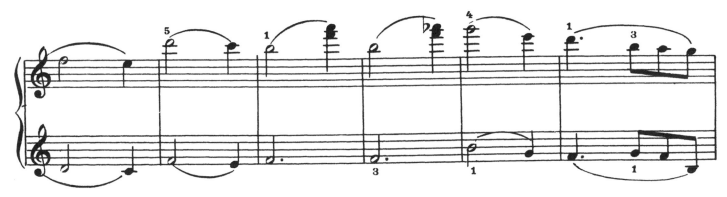

Secondo

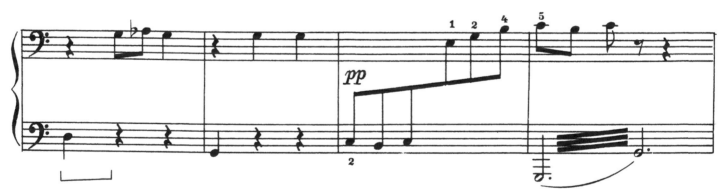

46963

Primo

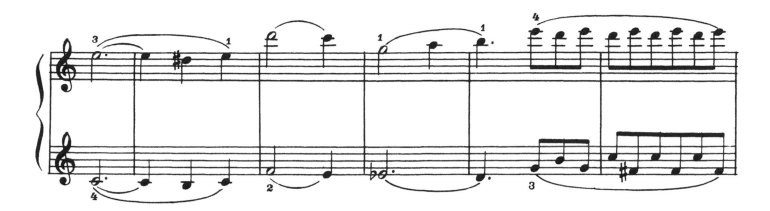

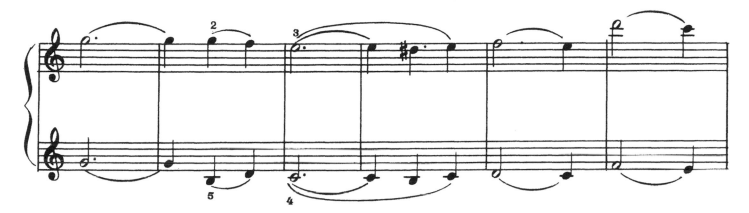

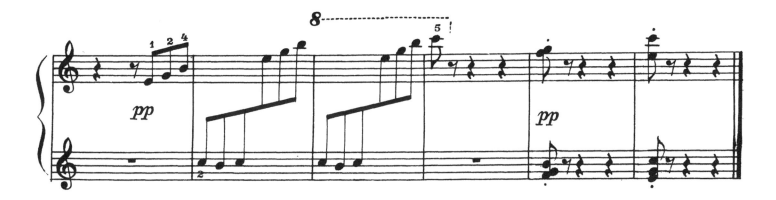

2. Polka

from a ballet suite

Secondo

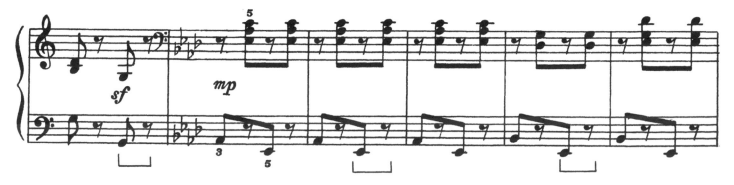

2. Polka

from a ballet suite

Primo

Secondo

Primo

Secondo

Primo

46963